for

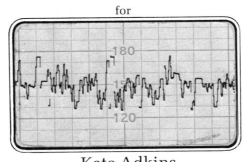

Kate Adkins

hello and goodbye, love.

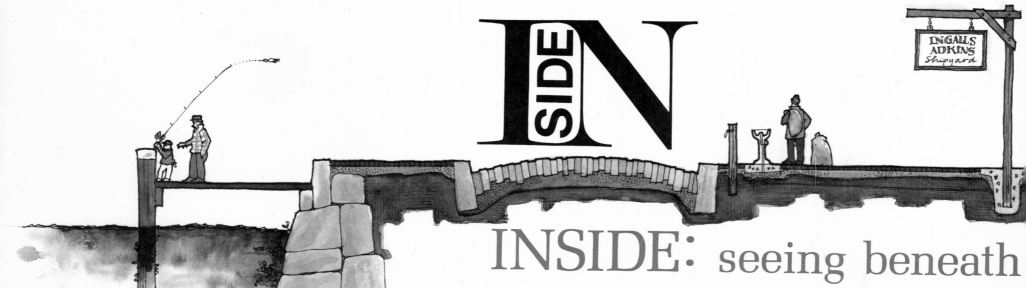

INSIDE: seeing beneath

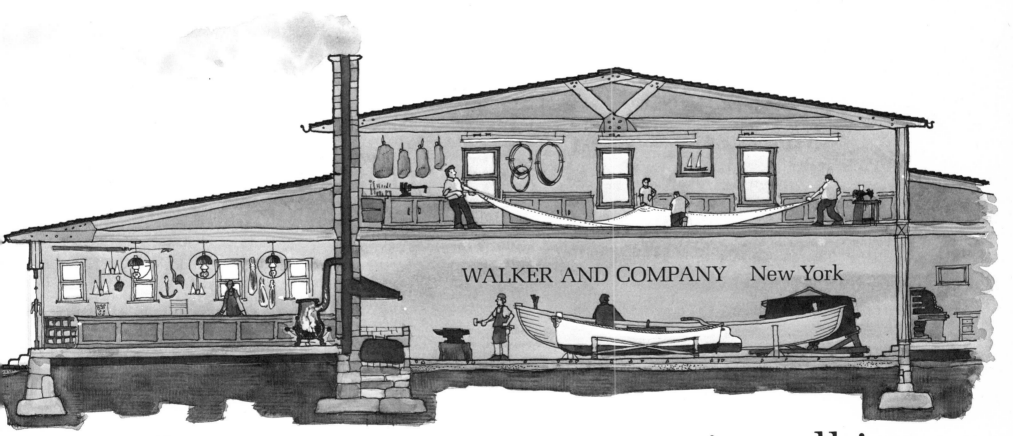

WALKER AND COMPANY    New York

the surface

written, designed, and illustrated by: **jan adkins**

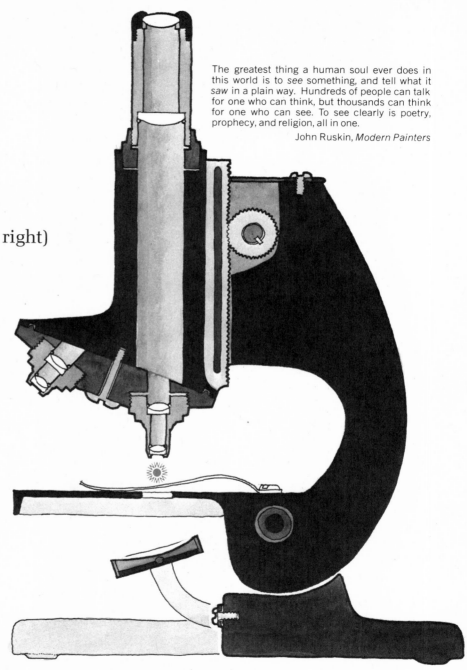

The greatest thing a human soul ever does in this world is to *see* something, and tell what it *saw* in a plain way. Hundreds of people can talk for one who can think, but thousands can think for one who can see. To see clearly is poetry, prophecy, and religion, all in one.

John Ruskin, *Modern Painters*

First published in the United States of America in 1975 by the Walker Publishing Company, and published simultaneously in Canada (up North) by Fitzhenry & Whiteside, Limited, Toronto.

Printed in the United States of America without Marty.

Library of Congress catalogue card number: 74-78108.

*Trade* ISBN: 0-8027-6193-3
*Reinforced* ISBN: 0-8027-6237-9

10 9 8 7 6 5 4 3 2 1

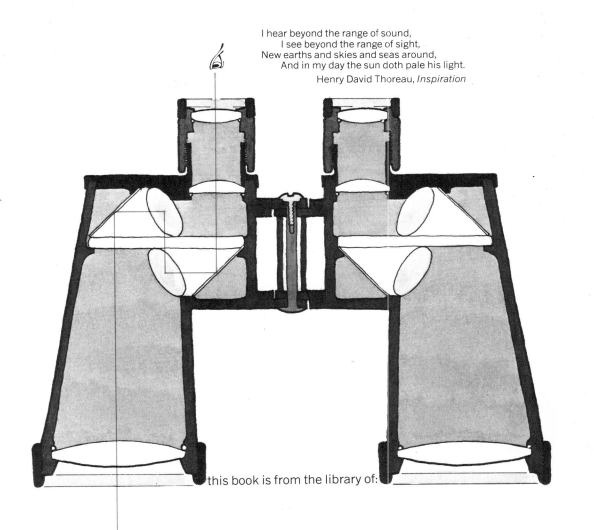

I hear beyond the range of sound,
I see beyond the range of sight,
New earths and skies and seas around,
And in my day the sun doth pale his light.

Henry David Thoreau, *Inspiration*

this book is from the library of: _____

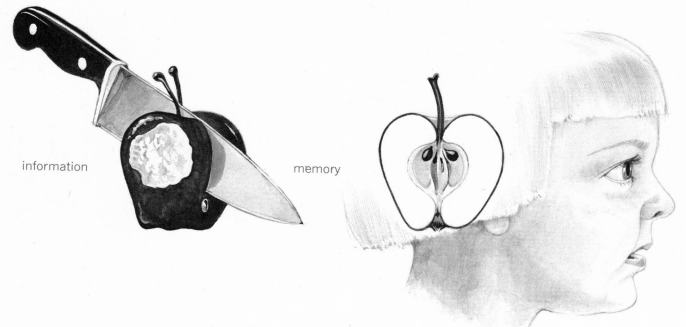

**apple** (ăp′ əl)*n.* 1. The round, firm fruit of a tree, the *Pyrus malus,* having a skin that is usually red but may be green or yellow [from Middle English *appel,* Old English *æppel.*]

information

memory

Your two eyes just *look,*

# Seeing

How do you see?

With your eyes, you say. Well, you are half right. With your eyes you see part of what's before you, but most of your seeing is done inside your head.

You see a round, red, slightly irregular *thing.* It has a brown rod or cord or stick or something coming out of a dimple in its top: that's what your eyes see. Back behind your eyes, your head is thinking over the information your eyes have sent it, and checking it against all your memories, working so fast you can't even hear it whiz. Before you can begin to wonder what

your head is doing, it tells you, "Nice work, you've found an *apple.*" Your eyes see a picture, something round and red, but the eye inside your head sees an apple.

How do you see? With three eyes: the two wonderful Looking Eyes set in your face, and with your Seeing Eye, a special eye inside your head.

You can eat the apple, peel and all, right down to the papery shell that surrounds the seeds in the core and gets stuck in your teeth. If you are not in a hurry you can break the core into pieces and see how the seeds fit and where the stem goes;

at shapes, colors, movements, but your inner eye *sees*, putting sense and sight together. A good word for sensible sight is *vision*.

and now your third eye really begins to work. Your looking eyes can only see the *outside* of an apple, but the third eye inside your head (since it now knows how the seeds lie and how the stem sits and how the papery shell surrounds them) can see the *inside* of an apple. Your third eye can see (or imagine, really, though seeing and imagining are very alike) an apple as if it were cut open with all its parts on display.

Your third eye can tell you how things are built, how things work, how to make a pie, why water bubbles out of the earth, what your wall is up to, and where your suitcase is while you are flying to Albuquerque.

Your third eye needs exercise. The more you use it the stronger it becomes and the more you can see. Using the third eye, the powerful and magical eye inside your head, can be a new way of seeing.

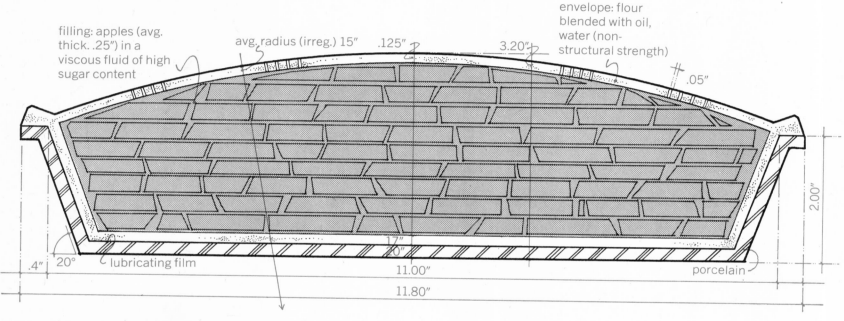

filling: apples (avg. thick. .25") in a viscous fluid of high sugar content

avg. radius (irreg.) 15"       .125"       3.20"

envelope: flour blended with oil, water (non-structural strength)

.05"

2.00"

17"
20°
11.00"
11.80"

.4"   20°   lubricating film

porcelain

Architects and engineers, drawing plans and construction details, use their third eye to see how their designs will look from above, from all the sides, and from inside. When they make a drawing of how something will look inside, they call it a *section*, as if they had cut a section out of a building with a sixty-foot bread knife and then drew it very precisely, measuring everything.

But it is not only architects and engineers who see things *in section* (this is their phrase for looking inside with their special eye). Doctors, sailors, geologists, and carpenters use that special vision. Cooks use their special vision, perhaps to see how they will make an apple pie.

If a cook and an engineer looked at the same apple pie, their third eyes might see it slightly differently. The cook would see it in terms of ingredients; the engineer in terms of measurements. They look at the same pie, but the eyes inside their heads do not see exactly alike. Your third eye is yours alone, and no one in this spinning, blue-oceaned world has one just like it. No one can see just like you.

The engineer has a trick or two for drawing his *sections* that helps him and may help you. The thickest lines are the outside surfaces of what he draws. The lines not quite as thick separate different materials. The blueprint of the pie, then, has for its boldest lines the top of the crust and the sides and bottom of

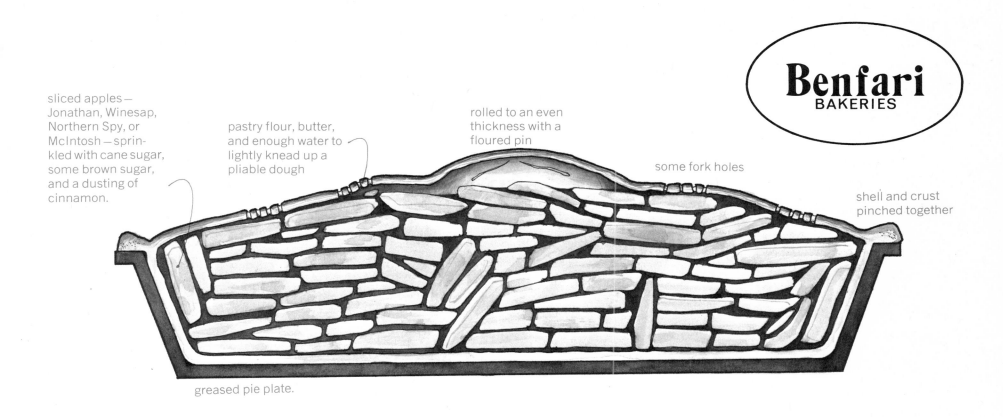

sliced apples—
Jonathan, Winesap,
Northern Spy, or
McIntosh—sprin-
kled with cane sugar,
some brown sugar,
and a dusting of
cinnamon.

pastry flour, butter,
and enough water to
lightly knead up a
pliable dough

rolled to an even
thickness with a
floured pin

some fork holes

shell and crust
pinched together

greased pie plate.

the pie plate.

A section can tell you how things are put together and what's inside them. The section through the pie tells you that the cook laid a flat sheet of dough in a greased pie plate to make a shell; he filled it with sliced apples sprinkled with sugar; he laid another sheet of dough over the shell and filling as a top crust, holing it with a fork so the steam could escape; he pinched the shell and top together to keep the sweet juices from bubbling out; and he brushed the top with milk, so it would turn golden in the oven. Now you know, and now you can make an apple pie. Why not?

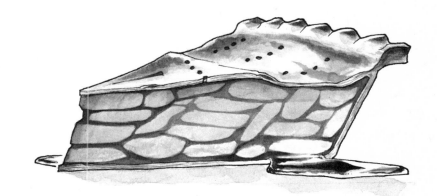

# the big sandwich

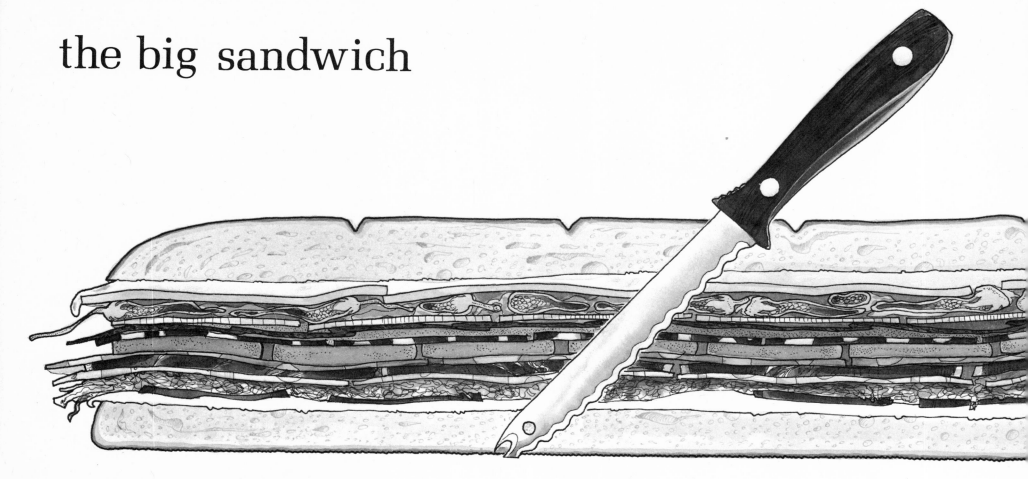

Your third eye can help you make plans. If you wanted to make a big sandwich, a really big sandwich, a Mount Everest or a Pacific Ocean of a sandwich, you would have to plan ahead. Big sandwiches are called heroes one place, grinders another place, submarines, or hoagies, or poor-boys, and they are all a major building project. Your third eye can tell you what to bring back from the store. You'll need a big bag for a length of crusty brown bread, great slabs of white and yellow cheese, cuts of salami, smoked ham, mortadella, blutwurst, braunschweiger, a head of lettuce for shredding, green peppers, pepperoncini toscani, a red onion, a soft brick of cream cheese, a jar of mayonnaise, cucumber pickles, and hot mustard.

Just as you slice the bread loaf two ways (horizontally to make a top and a bottom, and vertically across it to make smaller pieces for eating), you can see sections from two directions—or three, or four, or from any direction. Sections through the hero in different directions will have different shapes.

Sections through a doughnut will look different, depending on the directions in which your third eye and your sixty-foot bread knife are working. The horizontal section will be a ring, and the vertical section will show the round shape the ring is made of. The two sections together will show you what a doughnut looks like inside and out; only one section might be

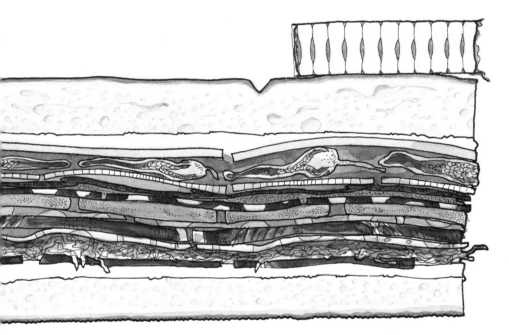

submarine roll
mayonnaise
longhorn cheese
pepperoncini
onion
salami
hot mustard
blutwurst
braunschweiger
mortadella
smoked ham
swiss cheese
shredded lettuce
green pepper
cream cheese
submarine roll

misleading. By itself, the horizontal section could show a round ring, but if the shape of the vertical sections were square, it would be an unlikely doughnut. The vertical section alone might be round, but if the horizontal section were oval, the doughnut would be stranger still.

With the information your looking eyes give it, your third eye can leap about to view things from many angles, outside and inside and upside-down. The more you exercise your special eye, the more agile it becomes, and soon it will be leaping all over, finding the secrets of simple things and the beauty of plain things.

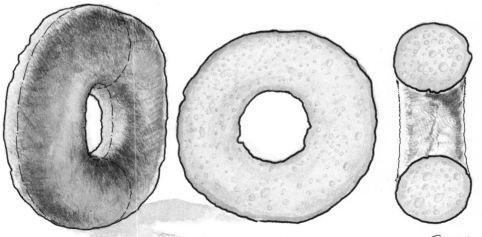

# pencil

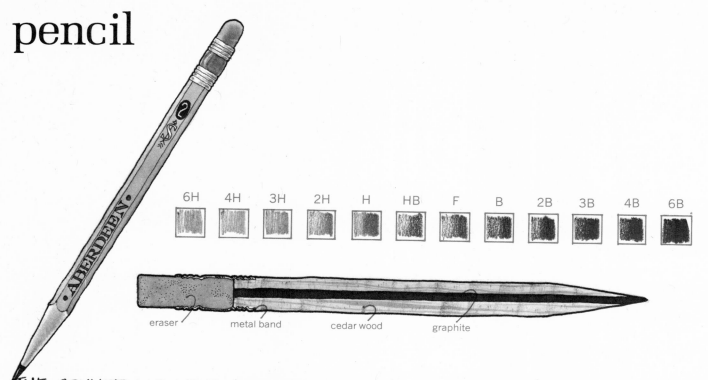

6H 4H 3H 2H H HB F B 2B 3B 4B 6B

eraser     metal band     cedar wood     graphite

THE COUNTRY IS MILD AND SANDY, NOW. WATER, IN MARSHES AND SLOW STREAMS AND CRAN

Unless you are very hungry your special eye will not confine itself to seeing food (although a delicious section through a well-stuffed turkey is always pleasant). Common things, the clutter and jumble that grow all through your life like friendly weeds, become interesting and worthy when seen by that magic sight; new character, new shapes, new strengths appear.

The lead pencil, that most common item, is stuck into shirt pockets and behind ears all over the world. Pencils fill up drawers and stand in sheaves beside telephones, find their way behind couch cushions, and ride over car visors. Seen in section, the pencil appears simple and honest, a basic idea, like the barn. Soft red cedar is used for pencils, and its sweet oil can be smelled in school pencil sharpeners everywhere. Two cedar halves are shaped and glued and clamped around a shaft of compressed graphite. The graphite can be hard or soft: it can be crumbly soft and deep black like the 6B lead, or go harder through 5B, 4B, 3B, 2B, B, F, to HB (which is medium hard and a dark grey), then harder to H, 2H, 3H, 4H, 5H, and finally 6H, which is as hard as a nail and makes a light grey mark. At the top of most pencils a metal band clamps on a pink rubber eraser. The wood around the brittle graphite (which is sometimes called "lead" because the earliest pencils were made with a soft lead writing core) gives it strength, and is cut away as the pencil wears back. The idea of the pencil is

# pen

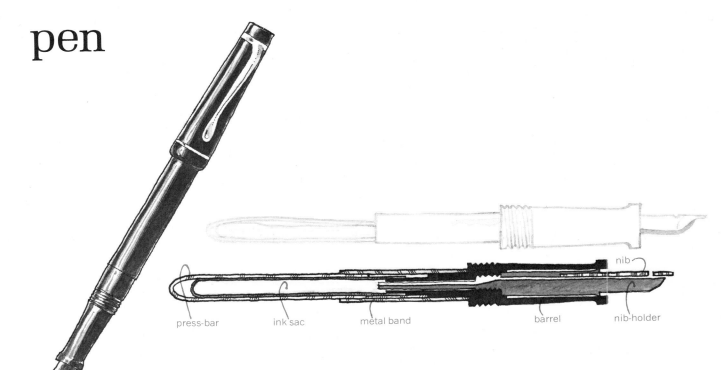

press-bar     ink sac     metal band     nib     barrel     nib-holder

BO SHAPE OUR COURSE MORE SURELY THAN THE RIDGES AND CANYONS OF THE MOUNTAINS WE HA
after our dinner had settled and the galley was clean we set a full press of sail to the light night

simple but sure. The pencil is not lasting but reliable.

Long ago a writer of letters, called a *scribe*, needed a deskful of equipment. First, he needed a quill-feather (one of the *primaries*, or flight feathers) from a goose or turkey. If he were right-handed, quills from the left wing of the bird were better—and more expensive—since they curved to the right out of the writer's way (left-curving quills tickled his nose). He needed a sharp knife to carve a writing point out of the feather's shank. He needed ink—wet in a bottle or dry in a stick to grind against a stone with water. When a scribe travelled, his tools were rolled in a parcel or packed in a case. When you travel, all the scribe's tools fit in your pocket, built into the fountain pen. In section, the fountain pen shows its reservoir of ink (a metal press-bar is squeezed and released to draw ink into the rubber ink sac), and a thin passage to the fountain pen's most important part, the writing point. The point is called a *nib* after an old word for a bird's beak. It is made of polished metal split lengthwise to lead the ink to the smooth tip. There is an elegance in the fountain pen's writing, its line varying thick and thin, and there is a kind of elegance in the easy flow of cool, dark ink from the reservoir into the curving nib and on to the thirsty paper.

13

# mechanical pencil

# felt·tip

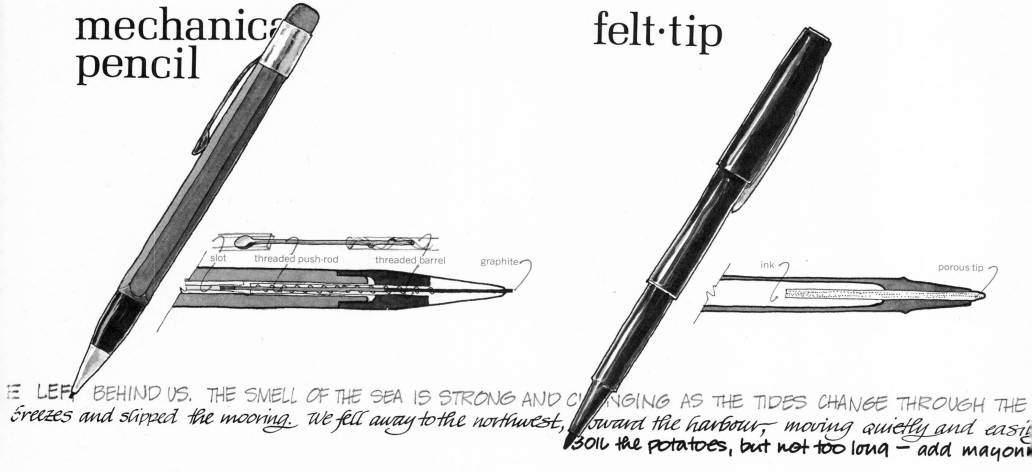

slot   threaded push-rod   threaded barrel   graphite

ink   porous tip

E LEFT BEHIND US. THE SMELL OF THE SEA IS STRONG AND CHANGING AS THE TIDES CHANGE THROUGH THE

breezes and slipped the mooring. We fell away to the northwest, toward the harbour, moving quietly and easi

Boil the potatoes, but not too long — add mayon

A section helps explain the mechanical pencil. Thin "lead" is dropped into a tube narrowed at one end just enough to grasp it. The lead is followed by a metal rod, flattened at one end and shaped at the middle to fit a thread cut around the lead-tube. When the point and body are joined, the flattened upper end fits into a flat slot running inside the body of the pencil. When the lead wears down you turn the point; the flat end does not turn, so the threads around the rod screw it down, forcing more lead out. The mechanical pencil in section has a queer, cog-work cleverness; it seems the sort of machine inventors and watchmakers might use to write down their lists.

The felt tip is quick and direct. In section it is nothing more than an ink reservoir and a fibrous shaft (of nylon or bamboo or balsa or any of many long-fibered materials) that sucks ink along to the point and leaves it on the page as it rushes on. It seems a pen for jotting, not for slow writing. When the ink is exhausted or the point wears away, most felt tips are thrown into the nearest wastebasket, probably on the run.

# ballpoint

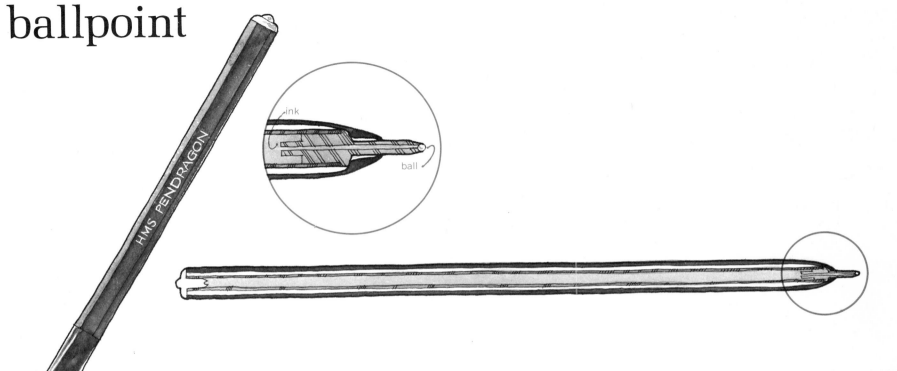

FROM T[    ]DARK SMELL OF LOW TIDE TO THE CLEAN EDGE OF HIGH TIDE, WHILE WE WALK BY THE SEA.
rough t[  ]black water — from one buoy to the next with the placid, turning compass and the bright, silent light.
:, minc[  ] parsley, celery, and onion, some red pepper relish (sweet), oil, vinegar, trace of garlic and toss.
$200.14 + 54.17 + 172.50 + 17.62 + 18.00 + 118.36 - 45.40 + 212.66 + 0.16 + 12.01 + 172.50 + 100.00 + 18.50 = $1051.22

The ball-point pen is a piece of precision technology, and like much technology it is a mixed blessing. The *tolerances* (the critical measurements) involved in making the little ball bearing and fitting it into the ink-filled tube's point are no more than a few thousandths of an inch. It is a precise and useful writing tool: its line width is thin and regular, good for making tiny legible figures in tiny accounting columns. It seems necessary to have ball-point pens in our age if only because they exert enough pressure to make good carbon copies. On the other hand, the ball-point does not write very beautifully, and it is difficult to "feel" the surface of the paper through the ball bearing on the end. The ball-point is a modern convenience whose use is so widespread that almost no one, now, has a handsome handwriting style.

Seeing common things with your third eye reveals more than just materials and workings. That magic eye inside your thinking head can see character, too: the pencil may be simple and honest, the fountain pen elegant, the mechanical pencil clever, the felt tip quick, the ball-point precise but suspect. What is most important for you to know is that the third eye sees more than *things*. It sees *ideas*.

15

# tree

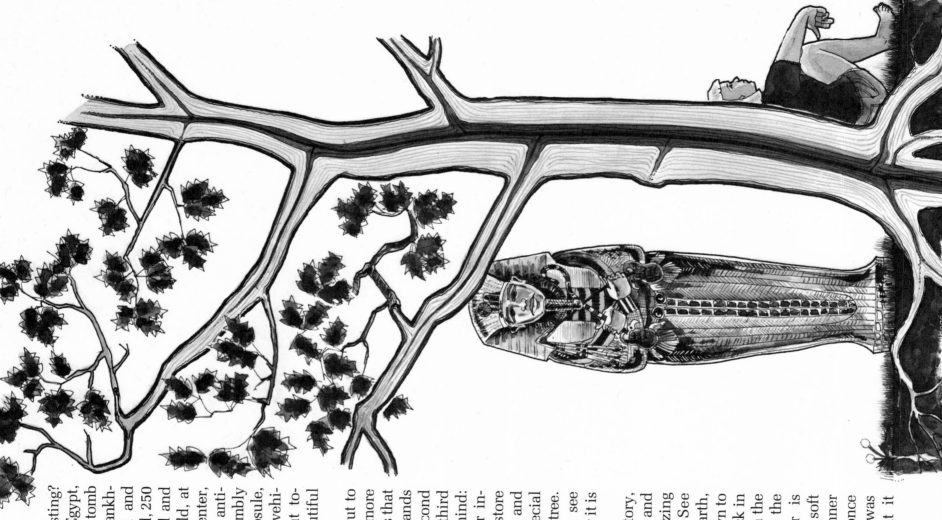

Just what is interesting? You could go to Cairo, Egypt, and be amazed by the tomb cover of Pharaoh Tutankhamen, three thousand and three hundred years old, 250 pounds of beaten gold and inlaid jewels. You could, at the Houston Space Center, watch the long, careful, antiseptic, controlled assembly of an Apollo space capsule, the most complicated vehicle men have ever put together with their beautiful hands. Very interesting.

Or you could walk out to a tree. Look at it with more than the two seeing eyes that have passed over thousands of trees without a second glance. Look with that third eye that is part of your mind: a mind that can gather information about trees, store it in memory vaults, and produce it when that special eye begins to peer at a tree. See more than a tree: see what the tree is and how it is and what it does.

See a great natural factory, a manufacturer of food and growth run by the blazing furnace of the sun. See down into the dark earth, twenty or thirty feet down to where the pale roots suck in water and minerals from the soil while they anchor the tree firmly. The water is drawn up through the soft sapwood. The darker inner core of heartwood was once sapwood when the tree was young and thinner; but it

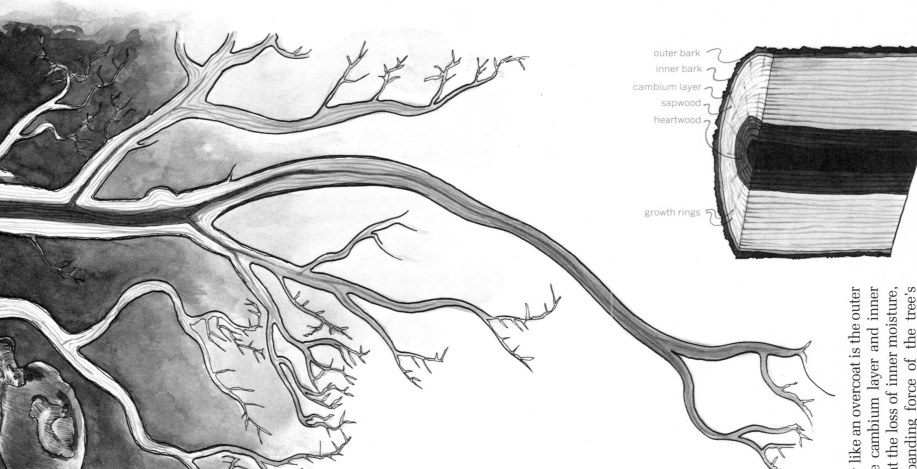

outer bark
inner bark
cambium layer
sapwood
heartwood

growth rings

has grown old, its cells have died and hardened, it is left as a post of strength within the tree. Water and minerals flow up the trunk and out the branches to the leaves, like water up a long straw.

Leaves are the real workshops of the factory. Given water, minerals, air and sunlight, they do what only green plants can do, make food. The leaves carry on a process called photosynthesis, putting together chemicals with the energy of sunlight to make food. The food, in the form of sugars, is for the tree's growth, and—if you eat walnuts or hazel nuts or pecans or almonds or filberts—for you.

The food is carried back down to other parts of the tree through the inner bark. The food is brought into the cells of the sapwood along the medullary rays. The food also fuels the cambium layer, an extremely thin layer of "growing cells" that expands outward leaving new sapwood cells inside it, making the tree grow thicker. In the warm, wet summer the cambium layer grows quickly, leaving large, light cells; during the fall its growth slows, forming tight, dark cells. This alternate quick and slow growth of the cambium makes the growth rings that appear on all lumber as grain.

Wrapped around all this activity like an overcoat is the outer bark, thick to protect the delicate cambium layer and inner bark from bumps, dense to prevent the loss of inner moisture, cracked and rough from the expanding force of the tree's powerful outward growth.

Look at a tree. Very interesting.

17

# airliner

Little things, big things. You might think twice before jumping from trees to airplanes, but it's no leap at all for your special eye, which can see little or see big with no trouble.

If you were flying to Mexico City you might go aboard this Douglas DC-9. Do you want a window seat? Very well, then, you are in seat 3-B (third back on the starboard side), 30,000 feet above the plains of Chihuahua. Forward in the nose the pilot, co-pilot and flight engineer are flying and navigating the aircraft from the cockpit, helped by instruments, radar, and radios banked against the hull and grouped under the cockpit. The power-assisted control cables stretch back over the main cabin ceiling and under its floor. At 30,000 feet the air outside the fuselage is cold (−50°F.) and not rich enough in oxygen to breathe. Forward, under the floor of the cabin are heaters and flasks of pressurized air. The wings that reach out and back are smooth and graceful outside, but inside are a complication of

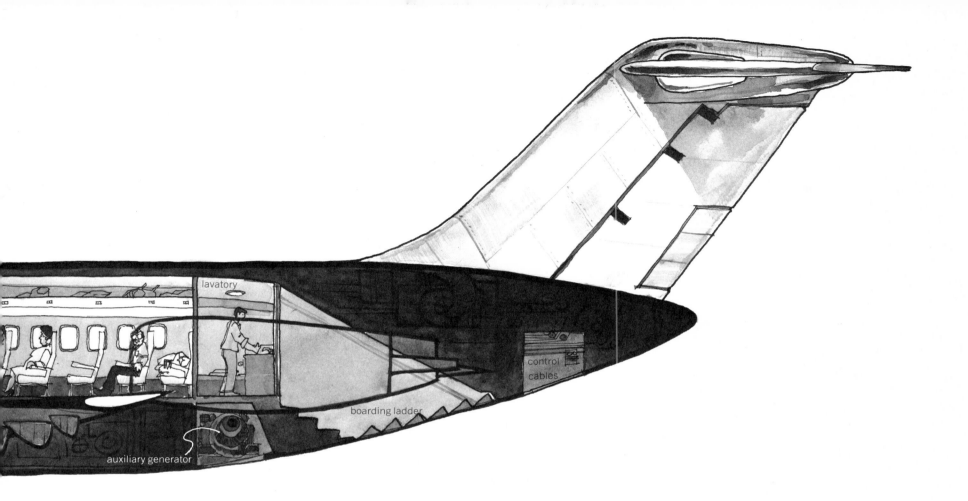

lavatory

control cables

boarding ladder

auxiliary generator

beams and bracing, control machinery, fire extinguishers, landing gear, landing lights and fuel tanks (6000 gallons of fuel, enough for 1400 miles of travel). Aft (toward the tail) are the lavatories, with supply and holding tanks for the chemical toilets near them. Forward is the galley, with storage ovens for the meals cooked on the ground and slipped up into the fuselage in aluminum cases by special trucks. Below the cabin floor is cargo space for your luggage, for air-mail, and for air-freight packages. Forty-five tons of machinery and 80 passengers flying at nearly 500 miles an hour over the plains of North Mexico: what Moses or Merlin would have thought of as great magic, we think of as common events, and we can charge the tickets on a credit card.

# the queen

steering gear  crew  tanks  laundry  library  boiler casing  boiler

Your third eye sees big things and sees little things. It can peer at the half-millimeter's worth of tail the mosquito carries, or examine the two-fathom (twelve-foot) tail that pushes the whale, or wonder about the two-million-mile tail of Haley's Comet. Seeing little and seeing big, your eye also sees the *relation* between little and big; it sees the size of one thing against another. This ability to compare the sizes of things is called a sense of *scale*.

The basic unit of scientific measurement is the *meter*, and the basic unit of your sense of scale is *you*. Your eye gauges everything around you by how much bigger than you or how much smaller than you it is. You can see yourself standing in your room, you can see yourself sitting in a bus, standing on a football field, wading at the edge of the ocean. You can see a horse standing beside you, a cat sitting in your lap, a mouse in your hand, a ladybug on your thumb. If Venus is 25 million miles away, you know that it must be very far, because you have walked one mile and know how far it seemed to you. A thousandth of an inch is small to you because you know how large an inch is. You are the measuring stick against which you gauge the world around you.

The *Queen Elizabeth II* is 963 feet long (you know how long a foot is, you know that a football field is 300 feet long). The bridge, from which the *QE2* is steered and navigated, is 100 feet above water level (as high as a ten-story building). She weighs as much as 72,222 Volkswagens. Using your special

signal deck
sport deck
boat deck
upper deck
quarter deck
one deck
two deck
three deck
four deck
five deck
six deck
seven deck
eight deck
deep tanks
double bottom

wheelhouse

theater

restaurant

kitchen    crew

cargo hatchway

crew

car lift

hospital

bow thrusters

fuel    and    water

eye's sense of scale, you can put yourself aboard the *QE2*, at the point of the bow on *one deck* with the water of the Caribbean Ocean hissing under you at 28 knots (about 32 miles an hour). You could walk aft on one deck and up the stairs to the *quarter deck*, and aft again—inside now—through the bakery and the main kitchen (150 feet long and 100 feet wide) and up the double escalator to the Brittania Restaurant on the *upper deck*, a room almost as long as a football field. Aft of the restaurant is a theater and a library; further aft is a great double room and a deck overlooking the *quarter deck* swimming pool and the *one deck* pool. Can you see yourself walking the length of the *Queen*? You can see yourself walking up the circular stair in the double room to the *boat deck*, for-

ward along the line of lifeboats and cruise boats outside the rows of shops, up to the radio room and the officers' lounge. There you could walk up to the *sport deck*, where the officers' rooms are, and where there are two large enclosed decks for games. Then you can ascend to the wheelhouse on the *signal deck*. One hundred and twenty-five feet below, 25 feet below the waterline, the ship's boilers are driving the great turbines that power the *Queen* with 110,000 shaft horsepower (as much as 1,294 VWs). The two propellors the turbines drive are as big as merry-go-rounds and much heavier—19 feet across and almost 32 tons each. Can you see yourself now, standing at the wheel of a Queen? What a fine eye!

# a house

It is wrong to talk about seeing as if it were easy. No; to see truly and to use your special eye is difficult and demanding, the hardest kind of skill to learn and the most complicated to use. As your two looking eyes must be provided with light to see, so your inner eye must be provided with its own illumination: it must have information.

You must gather information from many sources to help your special eye to see: from looking, from reading, and from asking (asking good questions takes just as much thought as answering them). Even with a hatful of information, seeing truly and well does not come easily. The mind behind your special eye must sort out what information is necessary and what is unneces-

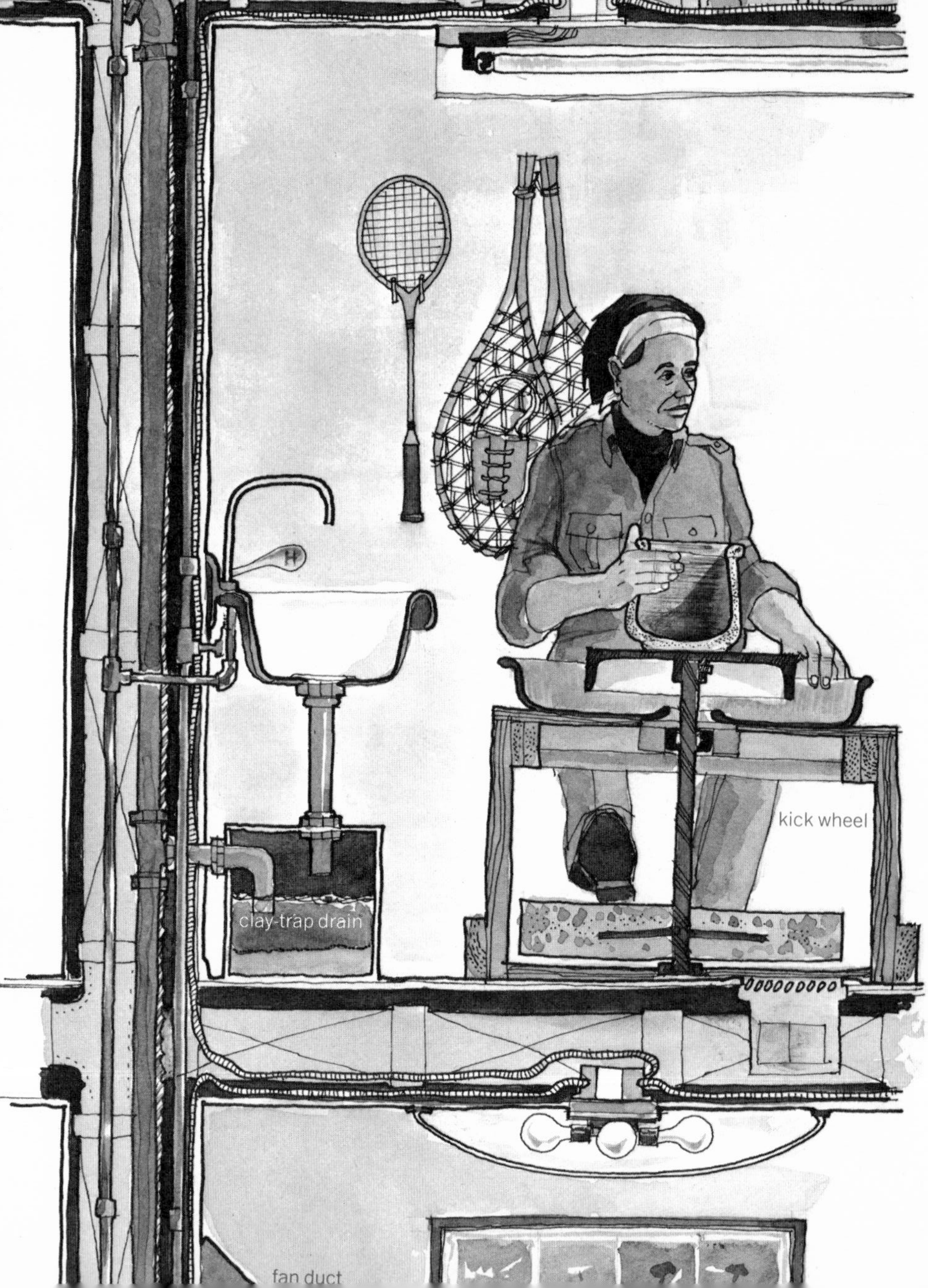

telephone line

author

kick wheel

clay trap drain

fan duct

22

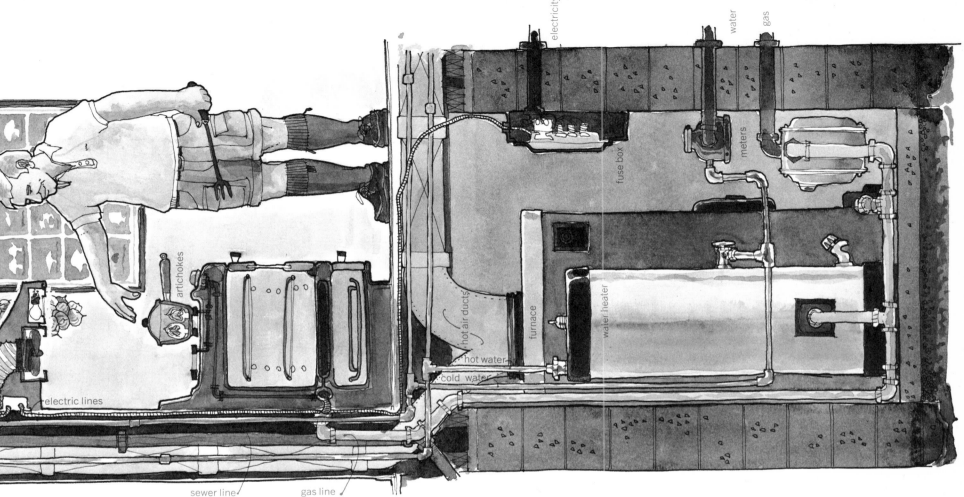

sary; then the special eye can combine the facts, put together the clues, mix the indications, add the feelings, and see.

What is blanker than a blank wall? To the weak looker it is a sheet of white, interesting only if it has a picture nailed to it; but to the strong looker a blank wall can be a challenge. Behind the strong look is a strong mind wanting to know what secrets, what energies, what common wonders would hide behind the blah-ness of a blank wall. The strong mind gathers information, eager as a hunting dog, and the eye begins to see, the wall begins to hum and drip and heat and talk. The eye sees now the web of electric lines entering through the fuse box and spreading through the house and erupting here and there as electric sockets or light fixtures. It sees the gas line entering to fuel the furnace, the furnace heating air and sending it through the sheet-metal hot air duct behind the blank wall. It sees the gas fueling the hot water heater; it sees hot water and cold water coursing through the walls in damp copper pipes. It sees the thin telephone wires. The strong look of the special eye sees the big cast iron sewer pipes draining the sinks and baths and toilets, and it sees the duct from the stove hood. It sees beyond the dull surface and into the lively core.

WATER TUNNEL

700'+

Have you ever seen a city street very early in the morning when there was no traffic, when no cars or trucks or busses passed by for minutes, when the street lay between its curbs like a river that had fallen asleep and stopped stock-still?

But a street is never really asleep. You may fall asleep on the couch and lie quietly without moving, but your heart is still thumping in your chest, your blood is still running under your skin, your lungs pulling in air, your stomach taking lunch apart. On the surface you are quiet, but under the surface you are a furious factory of activity, going about the business of living. The street may be quiet on the surface, but under the asphalt it is rushing and humming, because the cars that drive on it are only a part of the traffic the street carries. Under the streets of the city is another city of energy which your third eye can see.

When you cross the street, what kind of world passes under you in the dark below the ground? It is a world of pipes and cables, of sewers and drains, long tunnels, train tracks, dark passages crowded with thousands of wires, of damp heat and high voltage. These are a few of the things that crowd the other city beneath the streets.

Most of the city's high voltage electricity is laid underground in special lean-and-oil-cased cables. There are many kinds of electric cables, from the huge 345,000 volt "backbone" cables to the 120 volt electric lines that come into your house.

Many kinds of waterlines lie beneath the street, too. Small lines that feed drinking water to buildings, thick mains that supply fire hydrants, and deepest of all (more than 700 feet below New York) the massive water tunnels that carry rivers of water for the city from distant reservoirs.

All the waste of the city must be carried safely away. Sewer lines run from each building to a main sewer, which runs to a larger intercept sewer, and finally to a sewage treatment plant. Storm sewers carry away the quick rush of rainwater and snow melt-off that waste sewers couldn't handle.

Each telephone call uses two small wires, and under the streets are hundreds of millions of wires to handle all the "hellos" and "good-byes" made every day. In the same channels that the telephone company digs for its lines, the city installs its own line to all the traffic lights, burglar alarms, fire alarm boxes, and police call boxes.

Gas lines are laid down very carefully in high-strength pipes. They supply the natural gas for heat and cooking. In most large cities steam is piped under the streets in heavy asbestos- and concrete-wrapped lines. The steam is produced at electric power plants, and it is mostly used to heat buildings.

Five cities in the United States have subway systems: Boston, Chicago, Cleveland, New York, and Philadelphia. New York alone has enough track under its streets to make a subway line to Indianapolis, Indiana. Not only subways rumble along underground, but in many places freights and passenger trains duck down into the dark city under the city.

# harbor

soft shell clams    quahogs    lobster    mussels    5    tautog

Your looking eyes are skillful and quick. They faithfully observe most of what passes before you day by day by day. Because there is so much to be seen, they can be excused for not catching every detail of passing life, and because life passes quickly by, it is understandable that your looking eyes glance over the surfaces of things without penetrating into the depth of detail beneath the surface. Your third eye, because it chooses what it will look at, has time to see beneath the surface.

Standing beside the dock, what do your looking eyes see? The dock, the tops of the pilings, some rocks, not much more. What does your third eye see? Beneath the surface, it sees a lively water world: water plants, water forests, water creatures.

You can see how things at the surface are held: the dock is held by the long pilings driven down into the harbor bottom; the boulders showing at the surface are slabs of rock resting on more rock below them; the buoys marking the deep, safe channels are held in place by heavy blocks of concrete buried in the

bottom; the dory is staked off the rocky shore on a loop of line the fisherman can pull back in to him.

Deer live in the hills. The groundhog makes a home on sunny fields. What lives in the water finds its depth and its own fields and forests. Soft shell clams and quahogs live in the sand. Blue mussels live in thick crowds on the pilings. Oysters grow on the rocks. Around the rocks, hiding in the rockweed and sea grass, the crabs look for their food. The dark, mottled tautog prowl around the deeper rocks, while on the bottom of the

channel sea robins and flounder nose through the current-swirled pebbles. Lobster find rock dens on the bottom, and conches crawl blindly over the timbers of an old wreck. Can your special eye see the current itself, kicking up the silt bottom, rushing past the mussel-crusted pilings, coming in with the tide so the lobster boat motoring out fights against the swift flow of the sea?

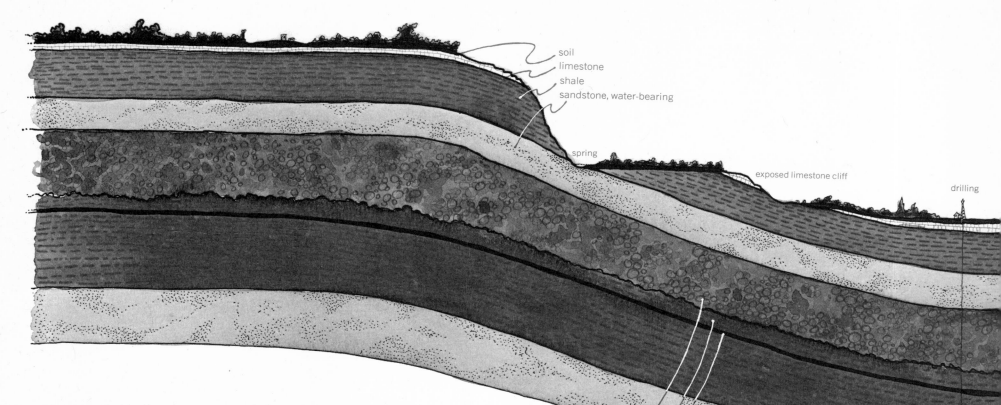

soil
limestone
shale
sandstone, water-bearing
spring
exposed limestone cliff
drilling
conglomerate
shale
coal seam
sandstone

Humans have little talent for satisfaction. Given a branch and some berries and a warm day of sun, the lark will sit and sing until the whippoorwill takes over on the night shift. To the tapir, puddling about the mud of South America, nothing is sweeter than his mud, nothing. The armadillo loves his barren desert and does not dream of cool gardens. But the human cannot be satisfied; men and women want more — the sunnier day, the greener grass, the hamburger deluxe.

And the human mind is not satisfied with a little knowledge; it desires whys and hows past all easy explanation. It looks at a yard and wonders what's beneath the grass, and deeper than that what is hidden? Deeper still, what is it like, what is beneath everything? Can the magic eye see the secrets of the earth?

This is a section through a valley formed millions of years ago when the crust of the young earth cracked. The break

shoved up a cliff and left a long depression beside it. You can see the *fault line* where the crack occurred and where the earth shifted, one side rising and the other side slumping down beside it. You can see how the layers of rocks once matched up. If you were standing in the forest opposite the cliffs you would be standing on the thin covering of loose earth, or *soil*. Beneath the soil is a hard layer of limestone, exposed and worn away

# valley

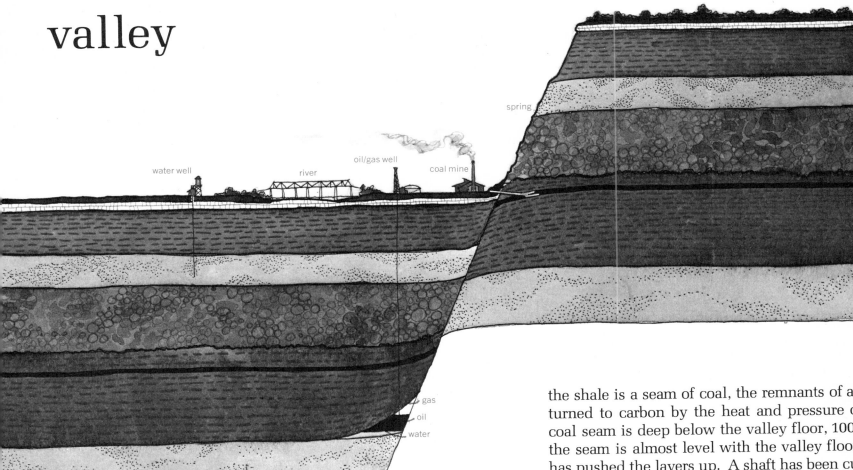

water well

river

oil/gas well

spring

coal mine

gas

oil

water

fault line

limestone
conglomerate
granite

on the shoulder and slope of the slump. Below the limestone is a layer of shale, also worn away by rain and wind. Farther down, a layer of porous sandstone carrying water: springs bubble out of the earth where the sandstone has been exposed on the hillside and on the cliffs. In the valley a water well has been drilled to the sandstone, 370 feet down. Down again, a layer of conglomerate over another shale layer, and lying in

the shale is a seam of coal, the remnants of a long-dead forest turned to carbon by the heat and pressure of the earth. The coal seam is deep below the valley floor, 1000 feet down, but the seam is almost level with the valley floor where the fault has pushed the layers up. A shaft has been cut in and the coal miners will work back into the cliff along the seam. Three hundred feet farther down, trapped in the porous rock 240 million years ago, is a black pocket of oil. Water lies below the oil and above it is a pocket of natural gas. The well on the cliff side of the river is sunk into the rich deposit, but the first well drilled on the other side missed and bored into the dark, uncertain earth until there was no hope of finding oil or gas or anything but granite and disappointment. The deepest of the samples brought up from the hole show the sandstone, the shale, the limestone, the conglomerate and, finally, hard granite—half a mile deep.

these heights and depths are greatly exaggerated

40 miles

3 miles

# our world

The eye inside your head, your special eye, is strong enough to be unafraid. There are things it cannot change, but there is nothing it cannot regard, nothing it can't look at with an honest mind. No one has ever looked at an atom, but men and women with strong third eyes have seen the structure of those tiny bits, ten-billionths of an inch big. No one has ever seen through the earth, but men and women with hunting-dog minds and vast imaginations have seen the world open like an apple.

They are not as sure of the world's section as they are of an apple's; there are parts inside its 7,927-mile diameter they can only guess at, but their lack of exact knowledge does not dismay them. Their lack of facts excites them. They send their eager, hunting minds out to gather more. They are excited by the chase.

They know that we live in a thin membrane of breathable air on a smooth-surfaced globe. If the earth were a ball one foot

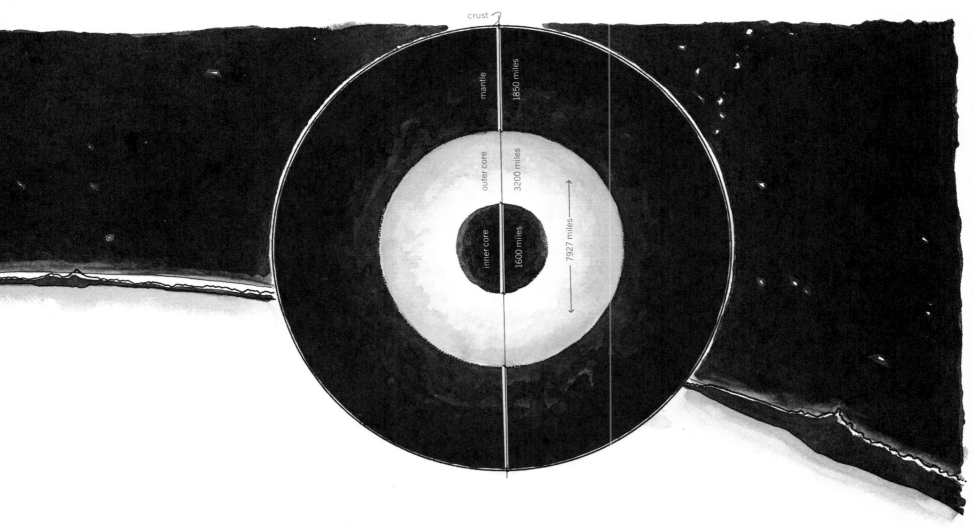

crust

mantle

1850 miles

outer core

3200 miles

inner core

1600 miles

7927 miles

in diameter, the peel of breathable air would be thinner than a coat of paint, and Mount Everest would rise to a majestic height of eight-thousandths of an inch—not enough to feel with your fingers.

They know that the earth spinning ponderously around the sun is not just a ball of dirt. We live at the surface on a *crust* of rock three to forty miles deep (thicker under the weight of the continents, thinner under the ocean). Beneath the crust is the *mantle*, a thick layer of heavy, iron-bearing rock reaching to a depth of about 1,850 miles. Further inward, an *outer core* of molten metal still hot from creation—probably iron and nickel to a depth of 3,200 miles—and at the center a 1,600-mile ball of solid iron and nickel.

Do they know it for sure? No, but their special eyes can see it as it probably is, as it might be, as it could be. Sometimes dreams and wonderings are as important as numbered facts.

A child is born, falling from warm, rocking sleep inside its mother into a terrifying place glaring with light (which the baby has never seen), howling with noise a hundred times harsher than the murmurings it may have heard inside its mother, and alive with the pains and shocks of hunger, cold, chafe, sickness. When a baby cries you must be kind and loving, remembering that its new eyes and its soft ears will need a long time to sort out its new world.

A baby grows and learns. Its eyes become quick and skillful at seeing movement and detail. It sees better and better as its expanding knowledge tells it what to look for. Its eyes see new detail and gauge depth and distance; its eyes grow stronger.

Inside, the third eye still sleeps, waiting for the looking eyes to learn their trade before it begins to exercise, too. It awakes, learns, and grows strong as it is used, grows to the borders of the imagination. It grows to the limit of *your* imagination and

not everyone's imagination, for if Copernicus's special eye had not grown beyond the limits of his friends' imaginations, how could he tell us what no one else believed, then, that the earth revolved around the sun? Leonardo da Vinci, Isaac Newton, Charles Darwin, Pablo Picasso: their inner eyes grew to fit the vastness of their imaginations.

A special eye: magical, eager, unafraid. It can peer beneath a city street or into a quiet tree. It can see character in a lead pencil and take an ocean-liner on at a glance. It can leap from a workboat on Buzzards Bay to an airplane over Mexico. It can leap from a round apple to the turning world. But what is the ultimate leap, the longest jump?

With a powerful inner eye, strong and agile from use, you can step into someone else's shoes and see the world from his eyes, from her point of view. It's a long jump, the longest, but you can make it.

**the end**